**CORNERSTONES OF FREEDOM**™

# The LEWIS & CLARK EXPEDITION

BY TERESA DOMNAUER

**CHILDREN'S P**

An Imprint of Schola

New York   Toronto   London   Auckland

Mexico City   New Delhi   Hong Kong

Danbury, Connecticut

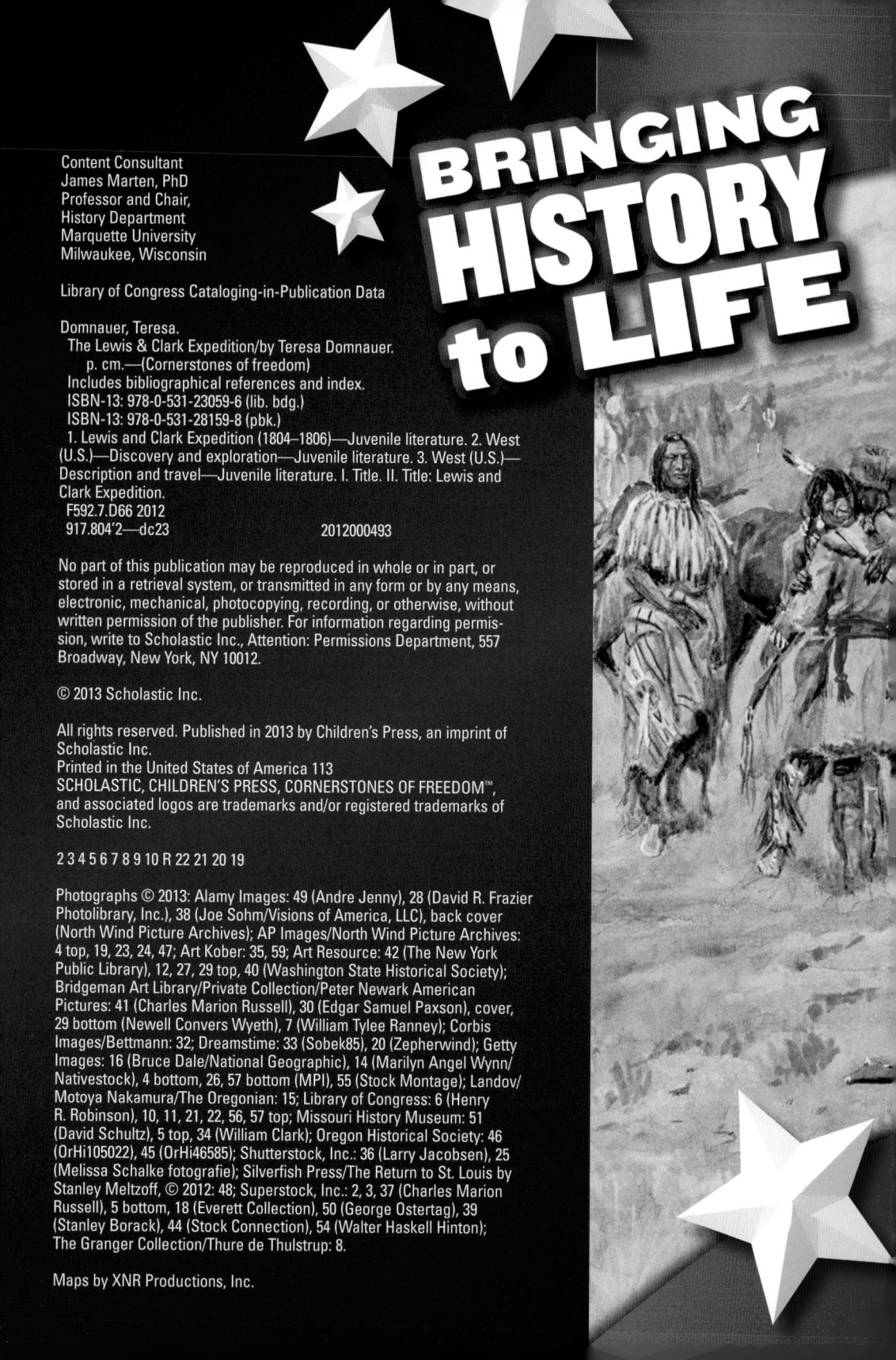

Content Consultant
James Marten, PhD
Professor and Chair,
History Department
Marquette University
Milwaukee, Wisconsin

Library of Congress Cataloging-in-Publication Data

Domnauer, Teresa.
  The Lewis & Clark Expedition/by Teresa Domnauer.
      p. cm.—(Cornerstones of freedom)
  Includes bibliographical references and index.
  ISBN-13: 978-0-531-23059-6 (lib. bdg.)
  ISBN-13: 978-0-531-28159-8 (pbk.)
  1. Lewis and Clark Expedition (1804–1806)—Juvenile literature. 2. West
(U.S.)—Discovery and exploration—Juvenile literature. 3. West (U.S.)—
Description and travel—Juvenile literature. I. Title. II. Title: Lewis and
Clark Expedition.
  F592.7.D66 2012
  917.804'2—dc23                          2012000493

Printed in the United States of America 113
SCHOLASTIC, CHILDREN'S PRESS, CORNERSTONES OF FREEDOM™,
and associated logos are trademarks and/or registered trademarks of
Scholastic Inc.

2 3 4 5 6 7 8 9 10 R 22 21 20 19

Photographs © 2013: Alamy Images: 49 (Andre Jenny), 28 (David R. Frazier
Photolibrary, Inc.), 38 (Joe Sohm/Visions of America, LLC), back cover
(North Wind Picture Archives); AP Images/North Wind Picture Archives:
4 top, 19, 23, 24, 47; Art Kober: 35, 59; Art Resource: 42 (The New York
Public Library), 12, 27, 29 top, 40 (Washington State Historical Society);
Bridgeman Art Library/Private Collection/Peter Newark American
Pictures: 41 (Charles Marion Russell), 30 (Edgar Samuel Paxson), cover,
29 bottom (Newell Convers Wyeth), 7 (William Tylee Ranney); Corbis
Images/Bettmann: 32; Dreamstime: 33 (Sobek85), 20 (Zepherwind); Getty
Images: 16 (Bruce Dale/National Geographic), 14 (Marilyn Angel Wynn/
Nativestock), 4 bottom, 26, 57 bottom (MPI), 55 (Stock Montage); Landov/
Motoya Nakamura/The Oregonian: 15; Library of Congress: 6 (Henry
R. Robinson), 10, 11, 21, 22, 56, 57 top; Missouri History Museum: 51
(David Schultz), 5 top, 34 (William Clark); Oregon Historical Society: 46
(OrHi105022), 45 (OrHi46585); Shutterstock, Inc.: 36 (Larry Jacobsen), 25
(Melissa Schalke fotografie); Silverfish Press/The Return to St. Louis by
Stanley Meltzoff, © 2012: 48; Superstock, Inc.: 2, 3, 37 (Charles Marion
Russell), 5 bottom, 18 (Everett Collection), 50 (George Ostertag), 39
(Stanley Borack), 44 (Stock Connection), 54 (Walter Haskell Hinton);
The Granger Collection/Thure de Thulstrup: 8.

Maps by XNR Productions, Inc.

**BRINGING HISTORY to LIFE**

# Did you know that studying history can be fun?

**BRING HISTORY TO LIFE** by becoming a history investigator. Examine the evidence (primary and secondary source materials); cross-examine the people and witnesses. Take a look at what was happening at the time—but be careful! What happened years ago might suddenly become incredibly interesting and change the way you think!

# Contents

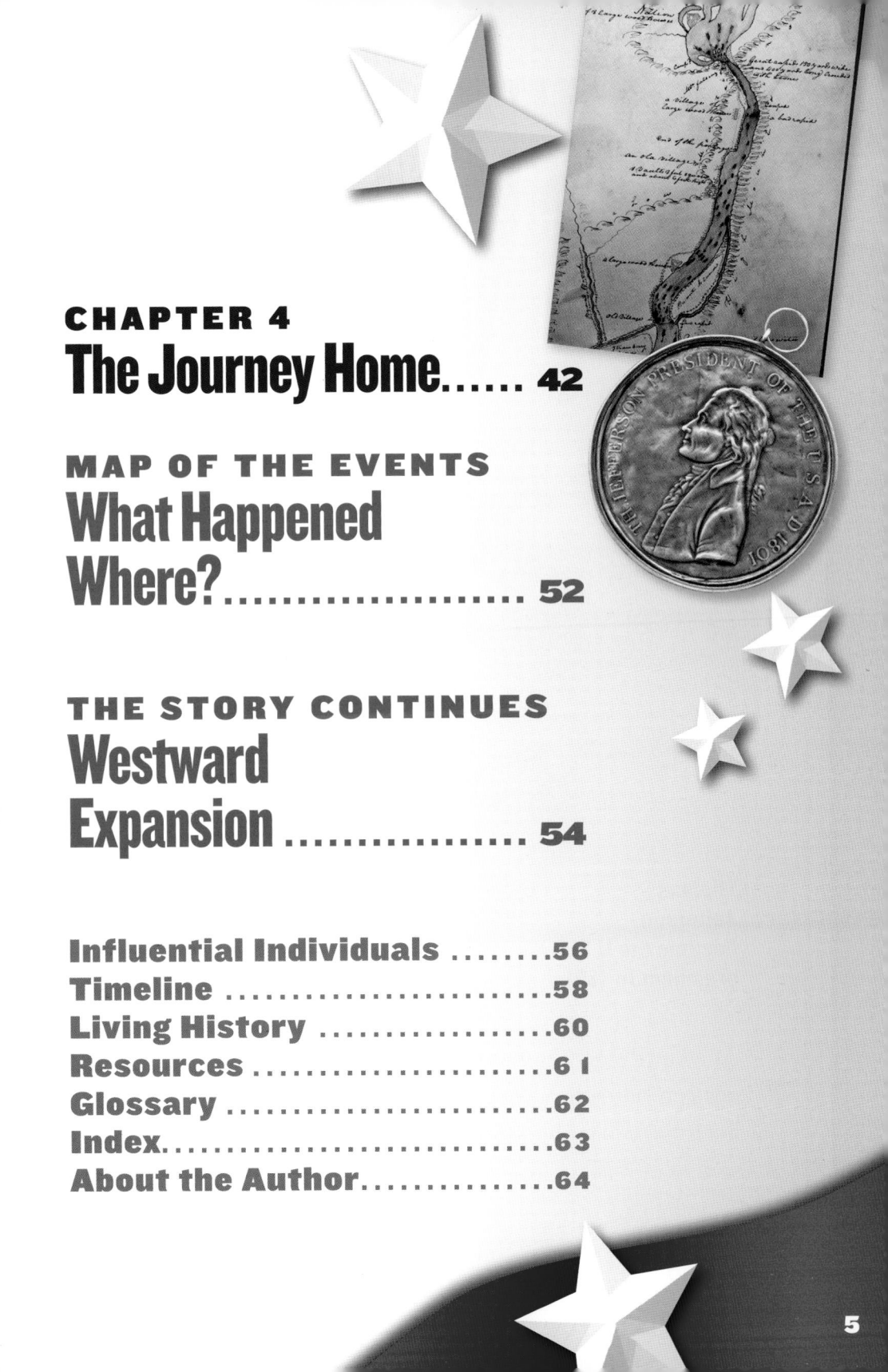

# The Uncharted West

**Thomas Jefferson became the U.S. president in 1801.**

The United States was still a young nation in 1803. Its eastern boundary was the Atlantic Ocean, and its western boundary was the Mississippi River. For 20 years, Thomas Jefferson had dreamed of the country expanding west.

**JEFFERSON FIRST ATTEMPTED TO**

As president, he now had the chance to make that dream come true. Jefferson wanted to find a route from the Mississippi River all the way to the Pacific Ocean. Such a route would open up trade with countries across the Pacific. This would give Americans more opportunities to gain wealth. Exploring new land would also give Americans more room to build new homes, farms, and businesses.

Native Americans had lived on these western lands for thousands of years. But few Americans other than adventurous fur traders and trappers had explored beyond the Mississippi River. A team of men called the Corps of Discovery would soon blaze a trail west through rugged land and across raging rivers. Their discoveries would change the nation forever.

**Trappers were among the few white men to set foot in the West before the Corps of Discovery explored the region.**

EXPLORE THE WEST IN 1783.

# CHAPTER 1

# PREPARING FOR THE EXPEDITION

The U.S. flag was first raised in New Orleans, the largest city in the Louisiana Territory, on December 20, 1803.

ON MAY 2, 1803, THE UNITED States bought 828,000 square miles (2,145,000 square kilometers) of land called the Louisiana Territory from France. The enormous piece of land stretched from the Mississippi River to the Rocky Mountains and from the Canadian border in the north to the Gulf of Mexico in the south. The deal was called the Louisiana Purchase, and it doubled the size of the United States.

## THOMAS JEFFERSON'S LETTER TO CONGRESS

On January 18, 1803, President Thomas Jefferson sent a message to Congress asking it to approve funding for the Lewis and Clark expedition. In his letter, Jefferson emphasized the potential for expanded trade, and Congress approved $2,500 to fund the expedition. See page 60 for a link to view the letter.

## Jefferson's Instructions

President Jefferson had many goals for the expedition. He wanted Lewis and Clark to keep detailed journals of the people, plants, and animals they encountered.

**Jefferson gave Lewis and Clark detailed instructions for the expedition.**

He wanted them to find the mysterious Northwest Passage. He also wanted them to create detailed maps of the routes they took west and to make friends with the Native Americans they met along the way.

## Preparations for the Expedition

Lewis had been preparing for the trip since Jefferson hired him in 1801. He dove further into preparations once Congress approved the expedition. He tried to learn everything he could about the West. He studied maps and read the journals of fur traders and trappers who had made their way up the Missouri River to what is now North Dakota. He also studied plants, animals, and medicine. Lewis had a boat built especially for the

## A VIEW FROM ABROAD

In the early 1800s, several European nations owned land in what is now the United States. France owned the land that the United States would gain in the Louisiana Purchase. Spain had a claim on the Southwest and parts of the South. Great Britain held Canada and part of what is now the northwestern United States. Spain and Britain were also trying to find a water route to the Pacific Ocean. The Spanish even tried to catch up to and stop the Corps of Discovery. Jefferson instructed Lewis and Clark to inform any foreign settlers and explorers that the Louisiana Purchase lands were now under the control of the United States.

**On their trip, Lewis and Clark brought a variety of equipment for mapmaking and navigation.**

expedition. It was called a **keelboat**, and it was 55 feet (17 meters) long. Lewis also purchased two smaller canoe-like riverboats called **pirogues**.

Lewis and Clark put together a team of rugged frontiersmen for the expedition. These men lacked discipline but had a variety of important abilities. Each man was chosen for his particular skills in areas such as woodcutting, blacksmithing, craftsmanship, and interpreting. The team included an African American man named York. He was Clark's servant. The full group consisted of about three dozen men and Lewis's dog, Seaman.

Lewis gathered a variety of supplies. He purchased tools such as a **sextant**, a telescope, a compass, and a thermometer. He also bought fishing equipment, cloth for tents, writing paper, and ink. He purchased beads, kettles, knives, and other items to give as gifts to the Native Americans they would meet on the trip. The Corps of Discovery also loaded the boats with medical supplies, guns, and a library of books.

SPOTLIGHT ON

### York

York was an enslaved man who belonged to William Clark's father. York and Clark had been childhood companions and still lived together at the time of the expedition. York was officially a servant to William Clark, but his role on the expedition was different. According to Clark's journals, York did many of the same jobs as the other men and was treated as an equal. Although he served equally with the other corps members, York did not receive payment or land after the journey, but the other men did. In fact, York remained a slave for 10 years after the expedition before Clark granted him his freedom.

# CHAPTER 2

# THE MISSOURI RIVER

The first part of the Lewis and Clark expedition consisted of a trip up the Mississippi River to where it meets the Missouri River.

ON MAY 14, 1804, THE CORPS of Discovery departed from Camp Wood near St. Louis, Missouri. The corps crossed the Mississippi River and headed north on the Missouri River. None of the men knew what to expect on the journey ahead. President Jefferson had told them to write down everything they saw.

Corps members often had to wade in the shallow water of the Missouri and pull the boat against the current. It was slow going, and after two months they were still in what today is the state of Missouri. Clark remained on the boat as he drew a map. Lewis walked along the shore to collect plant and soil samples.

## Early Encounters

The Corps of Discovery had its first encounter with Native Americans on August 2, 1804. The Native Americans and the corps members greeted each other and exchanged

**Lewis and Clark gave peace medals to the Native Americans they met as a sign of friendship.**

**Most native groups welcomed the corps members and their promises of trade with the United States.**

gifts. Thus, Lewis and Clark began a tradition that they continued whenever they met new Native American groups. They gave the native people peace medals that looked like large coins with Thomas Jefferson's picture on them. They gave speeches and fired their guns. They told the Native Americans that the land they stood upon now belonged to the United States and that their new leader was President Thomas Jefferson. Lewis and Clark would encounter nearly 50 different Native American nations on their journey.

Corps member Sergeant Charles Floyd became sick toward the end of July. The team believed that he had a

**The members of the corps were amazed at the bison and other wildlife they first encountered on the Great Plains.**

stomach ailment. It was most likely a burst appendix. Floyd died on August 20, 1804. He was the only member of the corps to die on the journey. The men of the corps buried him with full military honors on a site they called Floyd's Bluff, near what is now Sioux City, Iowa.

The scenery began to change dramatically in early September 1804. Huge, rolling, treeless prairies lay

The detailed journals of Lewis and Clark are still read and studied today. These journals tell us exactly what happened on the expedition from day to day. See page 60 for a link to view a searchable database of the journals.

before the Corps of Discovery. These prairies were far bigger than any meadow the men had seen back East. The corps had arrived at the Great Plains. Lewis recorded the beauty of these grasslands in his journal. He also wrote about all the new animals they saw, including massive bison and tiny yapping prairie dogs.

## A Tense Meeting

Lewis and Clark knew of a fierce Native American group called the Teton Sioux that lived along the Missouri

**The Teton Sioux had a reputation for fighting white explorers.**

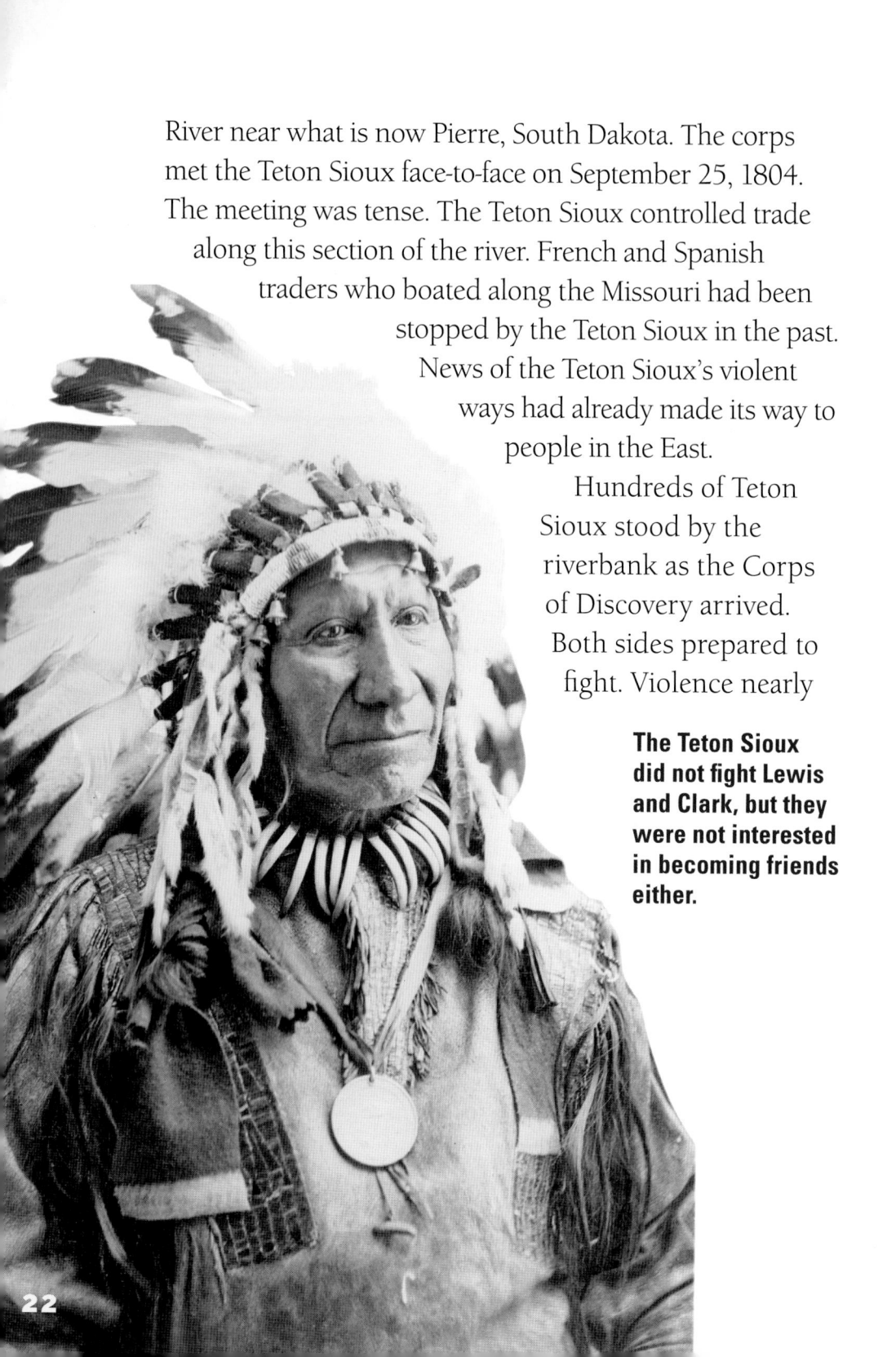

River near what is now Pierre, South Dakota. The corps met the Teton Sioux face-to-face on September 25, 1804. The meeting was tense. The Teton Sioux controlled trade along this section of the river. French and Spanish traders who boated along the Missouri had been stopped by the Teton Sioux in the past. News of the Teton Sioux's violent ways had already made its way to people in the East.

Hundreds of Teton Sioux stood by the riverbank as the Corps of Discovery arrived. Both sides prepared to fight. Violence nearly

**The Teton Sioux did not fight Lewis and Clark, but they were not interested in becoming friends either.**

**The Mandan lived in small, dome-shaped homes called earth lodges.**

broke out, but the Teton Sioux leader stepped in, and both sides put down their weapons. Lewis and Clark knew that the Teton Sioux could be a dangerous enemy. They had hoped to establish peaceful relations with them. The corps camped in Teton Sioux territory for three days, but they did not succeed in making friends with them.

## Friends in the Mandan Village

Winter was now coming quickly, and the corps hoped to cover as many miles as they could before the river froze. In October 1804, they arrived at the villages of the Mandan and Hidatsa peoples in what is now Bismarck,

**The corps members built Fort Mandan using tools they had brought from St. Louis.**

North Dakota. The men had been traveling for five months. It was time for them to settle down for their first winter on the trail. There were around 4,500 native people living in five villages. This was more people than lived in St. Louis at the time.

Unlike the Teton Sioux, the Mandan and Hidatsa Indians were friendly. They welcomed the corps and let the men build a fort on the other side of the river. The corps was not the first group of white men to arrive there. French, Spanish, and British explorers had also stopped at the villages as they searched for the Northwest Passage.

## Winter at Fort Mandan

It was a long, extremely cold winter at Fort Mandan. Temperatures dipped as low as -45 degrees Fahrenheit (-43 degrees Celsius). The corps members spent their time repairing equipment and writing a report to send back to President Jefferson. One corps member with blacksmithing skills set up shop at the fort. He made tools and other items to trade with the Mandan and Hidatsa for their food crops.

Corps member Pierre Cruzatte played the fiddle and the men danced. They learned as much as they could from their new Mandan and Hidatsa friends.

## TODAY'S PERSPECTIVE

Historians estimate that there were about 60 million bison (sometimes called buffalo) living in the western prairies at the time of the corps's journey. By 1905, fewer than 300 of the animals remained. Drought, disease, and competition for food all led to the bison's decline. Another major factor was overhunting of the bison for their hides. The thick, furry hides were used to make valuable coats called bison robes throughout the mid-1800s. In 1905, the American Bison Society was formed to help protect the bison population. Today, there are approximately 250,000 bison in the United States.

## A Translating Team

Lewis and Clark met a French Canadian fur trapper named Toussaint Charbonneau in November 1804. Charbonneau had been living among the Mandan and Hidatsa villages for several years. He had two Native American wives. One was expecting a baby. Her name was Sacagawea, and she was 16 years old. She came from the Lemhi Shoshone tribe. She had been kidnapped by Hidatsas when she was 12 years old and had lived with them ever since.

Sacagawea spoke both the Hidatsa and Shoshone languages. Charbonneau spoke Hidatsa and French. Lewis and Clark hired the two as **interpreters** for the Corps of Discovery. Corps member

Sacagawea's skill as a translator made her an important member of the corps.

**Toussaint Charbonneau (left) had been living among the Hidatsa and Mandan peoples for several years when he met Lewis and Clark.**

Francois Labiche spoke French and English. Sacagawea, Charbonneau, and Labiche together formed a translation chain. The corps needed horses for the rough mountain crossing ahead. The Shoshone people had many horses. The new interpreters were key to the corps getting the horses they needed.

**Many places visited by the Corps of Discovery now have statues of Sacagawea, honoring her contribution to the expedition.**

## Sacagawea

In bitter cold February, Sacagawea suffered through the long, painful delivery of her baby boy. She named him Jean Baptiste Charbonneau. Lewis had been practicing his newly learned medical skills with the Native Americans, and he assisted with the delivery. He wanted to make sure that Sacagawea stayed safe and healthy so she could accompany them on their journey.

Sacagawea would travel the entire trip with her infant son. The presence of a woman and a child made it clear to Native Americans that the corps was not a war party. Sacagawea served as both a translator and a guide. She found plants for the men to eat and use as natural medicines to treat their minor illnesses.

**Sacagawea sometimes recognized important landmarks, which helped the corps travel through uncharted areas.**

### Jean Baptiste Charbonneau

Jean Baptiste Charbonneau was the son of Sacagawea and Toussaint Charbonneau. He was only a few months old when he became part of the Corps of Discovery. William Clark became very attached to him and nicknamed him Pomp and Pompey. In 1811, Clark sent him to school in St. Louis. Jean Baptiste returned to frontier life after his schooling. He then traveled to Germany and lived there for six years. Upon returning from Germany, Jean Baptiste once again wanted to live on the frontier. He headed to California during the gold rush of the mid-1800s.

# CHAPTER 3

# CROSSING THE ROCKIES

Lewis and Clark developed close friendships with their translators.

THE ICE ON THE MISSOURI
River finally melted in April 1805. The corps soon
prepared to set out from Fort Mandan. On April 7,
a keelboat and a dozen men were sent back to St.
Louis. The boat carried plant, animal, and mineral
**specimens**, as well as maps and letters to inform
President Jefferson of their progress.

The remaining 33 members of the corps
continued up the Missouri with six long dugout
canoes and the two pirogues. Charbonneau,
Sacagawea, and baby Jean Baptiste were now an
official part of the corps. Lewis and Clark's men
knew each other well by this time. They had become
more disciplined compared to the rough-and-tumble
men they were when they started out.

**Grizzly bears proved to be more frightening than Lewis had expected.**

## The Rockies in View

The corps arrived at the mouth of the Yellowstone River in what is now North Dakota on April 25, 1805. Four days later, Lewis and some of his men came face-to-face with a grizzly bear. One of the fierce grizzlies chased Lewis about 240 feet (73 m) before one of the men could shoot it dead.

In early May, Charbonneau lost control of one of the pirogues when a strong gust of wind caused the boat to overturn. Important supplies and journals fell into the river. Sacagawea stayed calm and pulled many of these items out of the water.

The Corps of Discovery saw the Rocky Mountains for the first time later that month. These giant mountains were unlike any that the men had seen in the East. Lewis was filled with joy. But the feeling didn't last long. He realized that the corps would have a challenge in crossing the steep and rocky peaks. Progress continued to be slow along the Missouri because the river was very shallow and filled with rocks, making boat travel difficult.

## A Fork in the River

The corps arrived at the fork of another river on June 2, 1805. Lewis wasn't sure which branch of the river was the Missouri. The northern branch of the river was muddy like the Missouri. The southern branch

### SPOTLIGHT ON

*Prairie Dogs*

Lewis and Clark recorded more than 100 different kinds of animals in their journals. They also collected specimens, both live and dead. One of the live animal specimens they caught was a prairie dog. The French called these animals "little dogs" because of the barking sound they make. In their journals, Lewis and Clark described spending hours trying to trap one. They finally managed to capture one and sent it east for President Jefferson and other Americans to see.

was clearer. Lewis and Clark thought that it was the southern branch they should take, but most of the corps members disagreed. Making the correct choice was very important. If they went the wrong way, the group might not be able to cross the mountains before winter.

The Hidatsas had told Lewis that they would come to a great waterfall along the Missouri River. Lewis knew that they would be going in the right direction if he

William Clark used careful measurements and compass readings to make maps of the Louisiana Territory and the corps's route. After the expedition, American pioneers heading west used Clark's maps as a guide. See page 60 for a link to view the maps online.

could find the falls. He explored the land and eventually found the falls along the southern branch of the river.

In June, the corps had to **portage** around what today is called the Great Falls. The men carried their supplies and canoes on foot. During this time, they trudged through terrible storms with harsh rain, wind, and hail. They faced more grizzly bears, and their legs were scraped by prickly cacti. They limped along on sore feet. The team left one pirogue behind when they were unable to carry it farther.

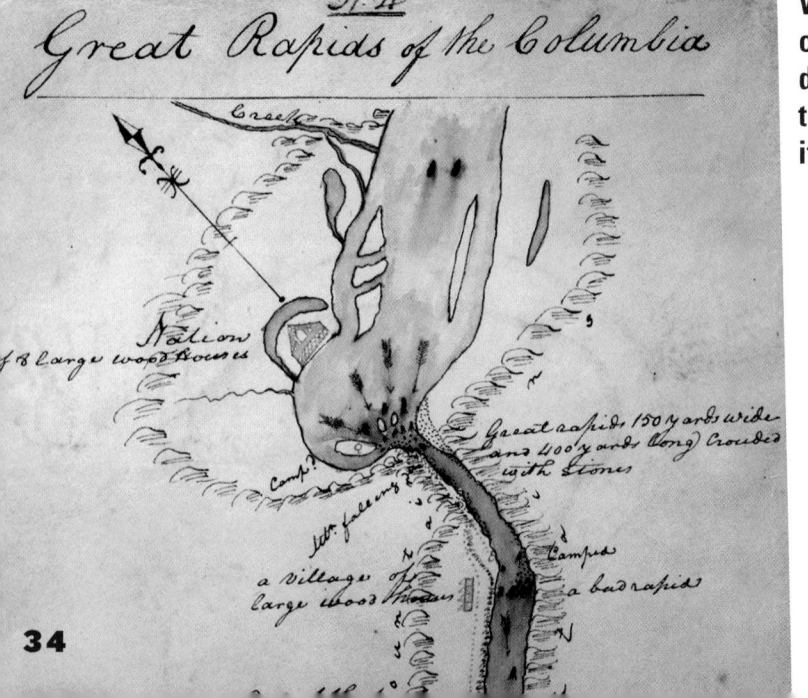

**William Clark created many detailed maps as the corps made its way west.**

**Portaging was extremely difficult because of the rough terrain.**

What Lewis and Clark thought would be a half-day hike turned out to take an entire month. When they finally made it around all of the falls, they were only 21 miles (34 km) upstream from where they had started a month before. The men made two more canoes so they could continue up the Missouri River.

## The End of the Missouri

The corps hoped to cross the Rockies before the winter. They were also anxious to find the Shoshones and trade for the horses they needed to make the mountain crossing. On July 27, 1805, the corps arrived at the Three Forks of the Missouri River, just south of what is now Helena, Montana. Sacagawea recognized familiar areas from her childhood.

**Lewis and Clark knew that winter weather would make crossing the Rocky Mountains impossible.**

The corps followed the fork of the river that headed west. The river was getting smaller and smaller. The men had to drag their canoes. It was snowing in the mountain peaks ahead. The party found the source of the Missouri River on August 12, 1805. Lewis and Clark began to realize that there was no Northwest Passage.

# The Great Horse People

Lewis once again scouted ahead and found some Shoshones on August 17. They led Lewis to their leader, Cameahwait. Lewis and Clark began to talk to Cameahwait about trading for horses. Sacagawea translated from Shoshone to Hidatsa. Charbonneau translated from Hidatsa to French. Finally, Labiche translated from French to English. Sacagawea soon realized that Cameahwait was her brother. She had not seen him for years and did not recognize him at first. They had a joyful reunion.

The Corps of Discovery paid a high cost for the horses they needed. Clark had to trade his knife, pistol, and ammunition for one animal.

**Lewis and Clark traded with the Shoshone to get new horses.**

37

## Across the Bitterroot Mountains

Cameahwait told Lewis and Clark of a route across the Rocky Mountains. The route would take them to the Clearwater River, near present-day Orofino, Idaho, and on to the **headwaters** of the Columbia River. The trail they would take was used by the Nez Perce people. It crossed the **Continental Divide**. Rivers flowed to the Atlantic Ocean on the east side of the Continental Divide. They flowed to the Pacific Ocean on the west side of the Continental Divide.

The corps set out on August 31 with 29 horses. Crossing this range of the Rockies would be the most difficult part of the journey. An elderly Native American man served as the guide. The corps members referred to him as Old Toby. Even with his knowledge of the trails, the party got lost for two days on the steep mountainsides.

**Cameahwait pointed the corps in the direction of the Clearwater River.**

They were surrounded by rugged peaks. Snow began to fall. There was no **game** to hunt in the mountains. The team members grew weaker and weaker. On the brink of starvation, they ate some of their horses. They then hiked 165 miles (266 km) in 11 days and emerged from the mountains into what is now the border between Idaho and Washington.

## The Nez Perce

The corps met the Nez Perce people at the Clearwater River. The Nez Perce fed the starving party members roots and dried salmon. The corps camped at the North Fork of the Clearwater River for two weeks. They built new canoes. The Nez Perce showed them their method of burning out the inside of the trees to make canoes. The

# YESTERDAY'S HEADLINES

The Shoshone people were mostly interested in trading their horses to Lewis and Clark for guns. Enemies of the Shoshone had obtained guns by trading with Canadian fur trappers. These Native Americans had used their new guns to force the Shoshone off the open plains and into the mountains. There, the Shoshone found only roots and berries to eat, rather than buffalo meat. The Shoshone risked being attacked when they tried to hunt buffalo on the plains. They believed guns would help them defend themselves so they could return to their home on the plains.

**The Nez Perce provided the corps with much-needed supplies and helpful advice.**

corps left their horses with the Nez Perce and set out on the Clearwater River.

## The Mighty Columbia River

The Corps of Discovery paddled the rapids of the Clearwater and Snake Rivers for nine days. The men arrived at the Columbia River on October 16, 1805. They had crossed the Continental Divide. The river current would finally be at their backs, pushing them westward. It would take them to the Pacific Ocean.

At the end of October, the party passed through the great **gorge** of the Columbia River. The environment around them had changed. There were large trees, thick forests, and waterfalls. The climate had also changed. They were now in a type of rain forest. The region was home to many Native American groups.

## "Ocean in View!"

Before long, Lewis and Clark could smell salty ocean water. Clark wrote "Ocean in view!" in his journal on November 7, 1805. But he wrote this too soon. They had merely come into an **estuary** of the river. They were still 20 miles (32 km) from the coast.

**As they traveled down the Columbia River and began smelling saltwater, the corps members knew that they were getting close to the Pacific coast.**

# CHAPTER 4

# THE JOURNEY HOME

More than a year after leaving St. Louis, the Corps of Discovery finally arrived at the Pacific Ocean.

ON NOVEMBER 18, 1805, William Clark spied the ocean from the top of a hill. The Corps of Discovery had made it to the Pacific. The team's trailblazing would forever change the United States. The men prepared to settle into camp at Fort Clatsop, named for a local native group, in what is now Oregon. They were as far from home as they could be. A long, wet winter lay ahead.

Today, a reconstructed version of Fort Clatsop exists as part of Fort Clatsop National Memorial in Oregon.

## Winter at Fort Clatsop

It rained almost every day during the winter. It was hard to keep a fire going because everything was always wet. The men ate elk for every meal. The corps members spent their time making **moccasins**, writing in their journals, and making maps. Lewis continued writing his descriptions of plants and animals. The corps had found 122 new **species** of animals and 178 of plants.

## Back over the Mountains

The Corps of Discovery departed Fort Clatsop on March 23, 1806, and gave the fort to the Clatsop Indians. The party now had to fight the Columbia's strong current and portage around its falls. The men were often bothered by the Chinookan people, who tried to steal their supplies. Finally, they gave up the canoes and set out on foot for the mountains. They camped with their Nez Perce friends until the weather improved.

The Chinookan people lived mainly along the Columbia River in what are now the states of Washington and Oregon.

### Sergeant Patrick Gass

Sergeant Patrick Gass was highly valued by the Corps of Discovery for his carpentry skills. He was a great help when it came to building the party's winter forts and dugout canoes. In 1807, Gass became the first corps member to publish his journal of the trip. He had the help of a book and stationery store owner named David McKeehan. McKeehan edited Gass's rough journal entries to make them easier to read. The name Corps of Discovery appeared on the title page of the journal, popularizing the term among those who read it.

They reached Travelers' Rest on June 30, 1806. Native Americans had long used this spot in present-day Montana as a meeting place and resting point. The next day, Lewis and Clark chose to split the group into three parties so they could explore more of the Louisiana Purchase. Lewis and nine of the men explored the Marias River to the north. Clark and his team paddled down the Yellowstone River to the south. Corps member Sergeant Patrick Gass led the remainder of the party in the portage around the Great Falls.

## Violent Encounters

Lewis had a violent encounter with the Piegan Blackfeet people on July 26, 1806. A Blackfoot man tried to steal rifles while Lewis's group was camping with them. Lewis shot and killed two Blackfeet in the scuffle that followed.

**Today, a re-creation of Fort Mandan stands near the original fort's location.**

Clark and his party ran into trouble, too. Crow Indians sometimes stole horses. Clark's group traveled through Crow territory on July 21, 1806. The men never saw a Crow Indian, but half of their horses were stolen.

The three parties met again on August 12 and continued their journey home. The current of the Missouri River would now swiftly carry them east.

## Saying Good-bye

The corps arrived back at Fort Mandan on August 17. They said farewell to Charbonneau, Sacagawea, and little Pompey.

The men once again faced the fierce Teton Sioux as they pressed homeward. Dozens of warriors lined the river as the corps went past. The Indians looked threatening but did not harm the party.

## A Hero's Welcome

The Corps of Discovery arrived in St. Louis on September 23, 1806. The return trip took only six months. They had been gone for a total of two years, four months, and

**The corps's return to St. Louis surprised many people, who believed Lewis and Clark were dead.**

**Statues of Lewis and Clark stand at several places along the route of their expedition.**

10 days. Many people back home had given them up for dead. They were greeted by thousands of excited citizens in St. Louis. Captains Lewis and Clark were honored in celebrations in Indiana and Kentucky as well. They were national heroes.

On November 19, 1805
Capt. William Clark
led a small party
along this beach.
This excursion was
their first contact
with the Pacific Ocean.

The following men
accompanied Capt. Clark:

Sgt. John Ordway
Sgt. Nathaniel Pryor
York
John Colter
Peter Weiser
Joseph Field
Reuben Field
George Shannon
William Bratton
Francois Labiche
Toussaint Charbonneau

**Monuments and historical markers allow tourists to find the exact locations where the corps traveled.**

## After the Voyage

There is no record of the first meeting between Meriwether Lewis and Thomas Jefferson after the expedition. Lewis was appointed governor of the Louisiana Territory soon after returning. But he soon began to have troubles. He couldn't

## A FIRSTHAND LOOK AT
## MERIWETHER LEWIS'S LETTER TO THOMAS JEFFERSON

Lewis wrote a letter to President Jefferson on September 23, 1806, to inform him of the successful completion of the expedition. The letter also explained that there was no Northwest Passage. See page 60 for a link to read text of the letter online.

govern the area properly. Lewis sank into a deep state of sadness and eventually took his own life in 1809. He never organized or published his journals.

After the expedition, William Clark received payment and land for his services to the Corps of Discovery. He adopted Jean Baptiste Charbonneau in 1811 when Toussaint Charbonneau and Sacagawea decided to return to frontier life. He was named governor of the Missouri Territory in 1813 and continued to update his maps as new information became available. In 1814 Clark published his and Lewis's journals, which are still studied today.

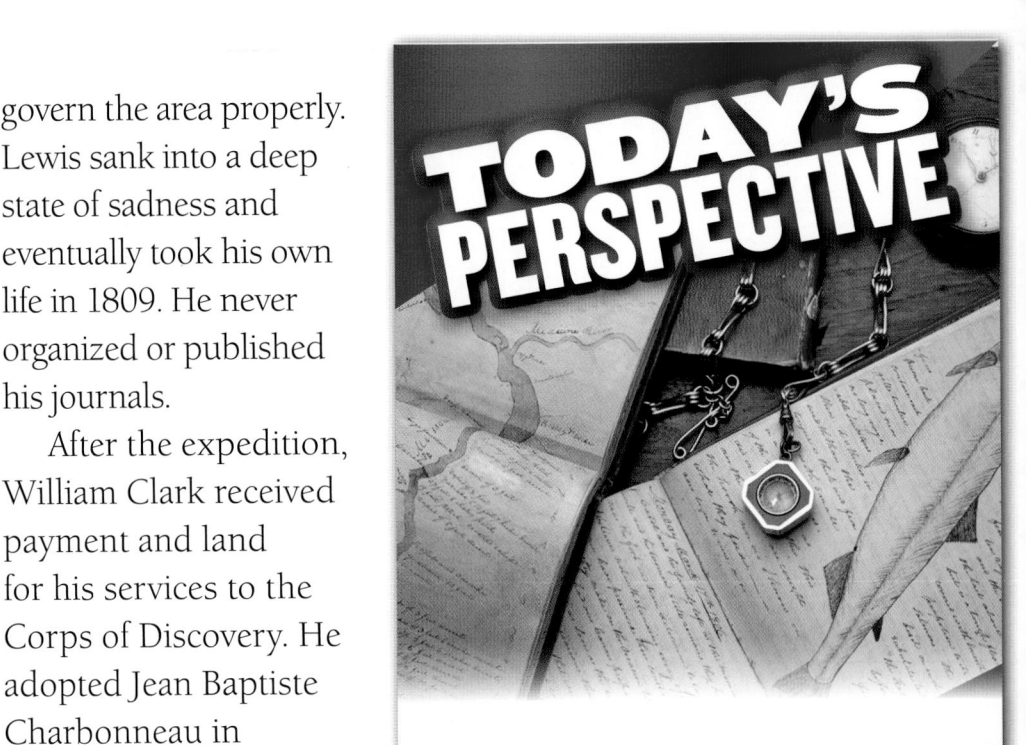

# TODAY'S PERSPECTIVE

Today, Lewis and Clark are still viewed as brave explorers and heroes. Their journey fascinates people of all ages. Items from Lewis and Clark's trip, such as their compass and drafting tools, are on display in museums across the country. Documents related to their trip have been preserved by the National Archives and the Library of Congress. Documentary filmmaker Ken Burns created a series about Lewis and Clark's journey. National Geographic produced a television special about the expedition. Many modern-day cities along Lewis and Clark's route hosted celebrations in honor of the 200th anniversary of the expedition.

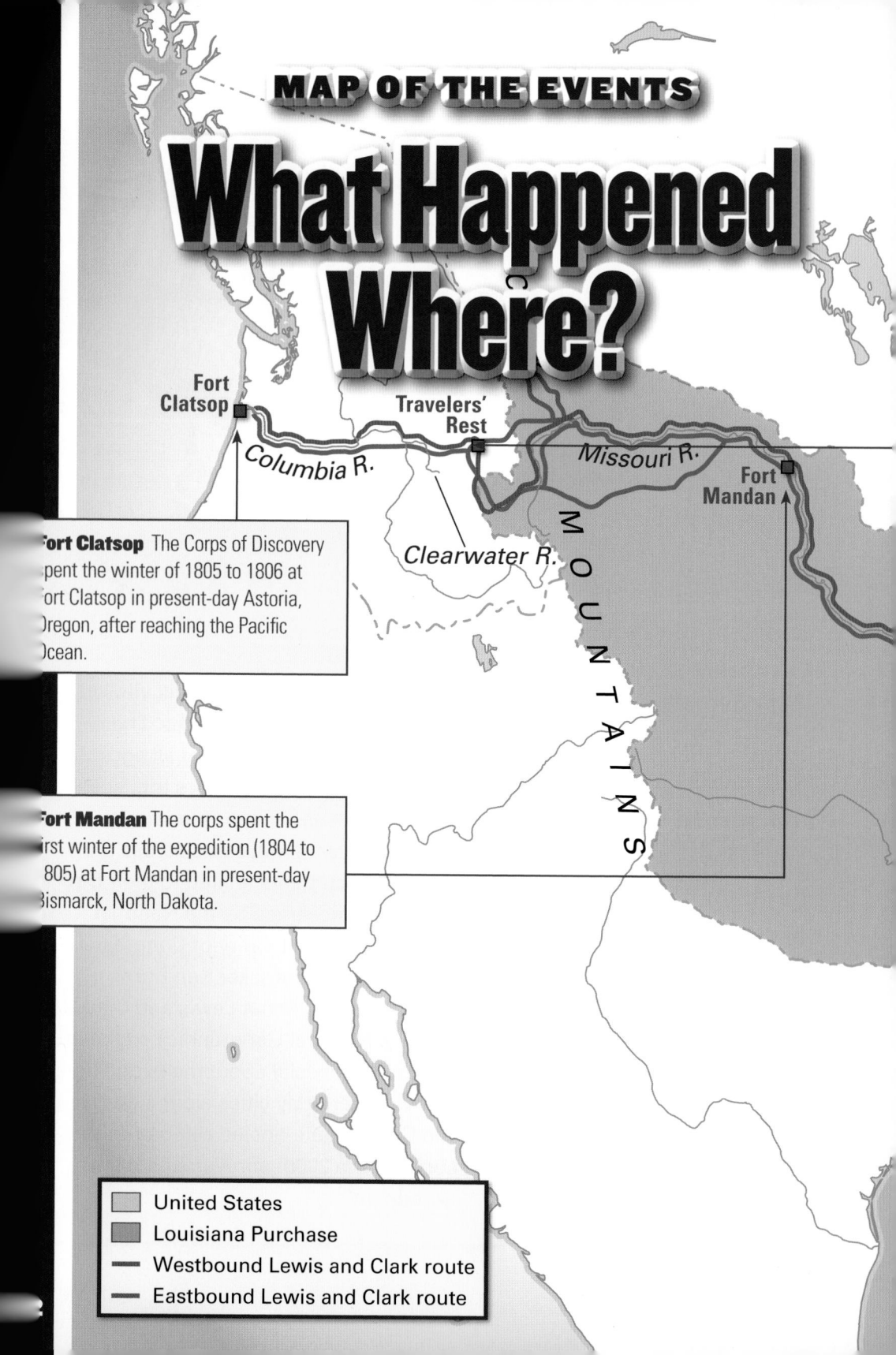

# MAP OF THE EVENTS

# What Happened Where?

**Fort Clatsop**

**Travelers' Rest**

Columbia R.

Missouri R.

**Fort Mandan**

Clearwater R.

M O U N T A I N S

**Fort Clatsop** The Corps of Discovery spent the winter of 1805 to 1806 at Fort Clatsop in present-day Astoria, Oregon, after reaching the Pacific Ocean.

**Fort Mandan** The corps spent the first winter of the expedition (1804 to 1805) at Fort Mandan in present-day Bismarck, North Dakota.

☐ United States
☐ Louisiana Purchase
— Westbound Lewis and Clark route
— Eastbound Lewis and Clark route

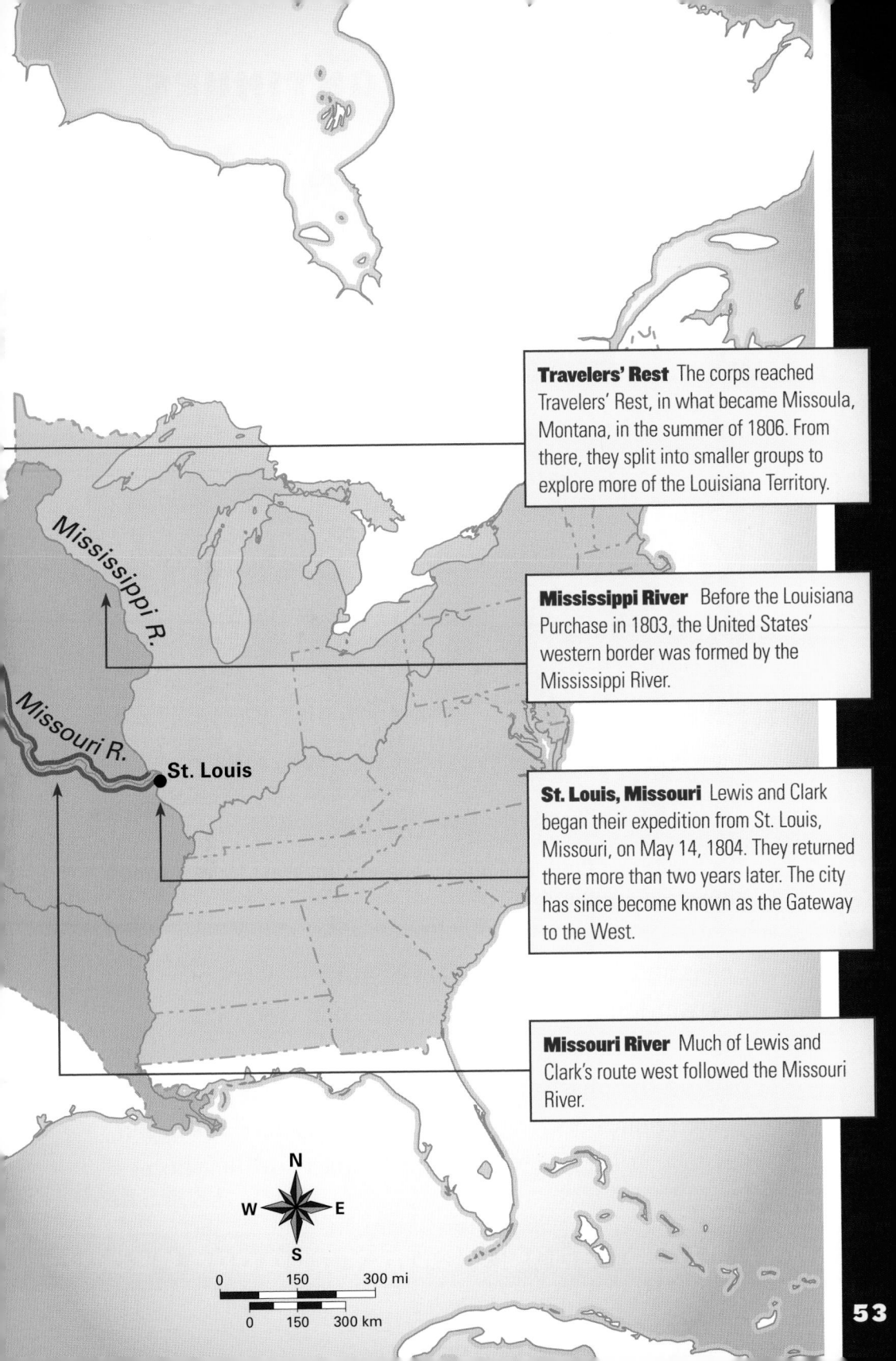

**Travelers' Rest** The corps reached Travelers' Rest, in what became Missoula, Montana, in the summer of 1806. From there, they split into smaller groups to explore more of the Louisiana Territory.

**Mississippi River** Before the Louisiana Purchase in 1803, the United States' western border was formed by the Mississippi River.

**St. Louis, Missouri** Lewis and Clark began their expedition from St. Louis, Missouri, on May 14, 1804. They returned there more than two years later. The city has since become known as the Gateway to the West.

**Missouri River** Much of Lewis and Clark's route west followed the Missouri River.

Mississippi R.

Missouri R.

St. Louis

N
W    E
S

0    150    300 mi

0    150    300 km

# Westward Expansion

**The Lewis and Clark expedition opened the West for thousands of American settlers.**

Lewis and Clark's expedition began a new era of westward movement in America. Their discoveries showed Thomas Jefferson and other Americans what lay beyond the Mississippi River. As the eastern part of the United States became more crowded, Americans began to move west. They wanted more space for their homes

**IN THE MID-1800S, NEARLY 300,000 PEOPLE**

and families and for farming. They would use Lewis and Clark's maps as a guide.

Americans would settle the lands of the Louisiana Purchase, which would make up all or part of 15 states. Cities, towns, and farms would soon cover the land. America would continue to expand to the southwest, west, and northwest. In 1848, gold was discovered in California, and thousands of people rushed to the area hoping to become rich. As Americans settled western lands, Native Americans were continually forced off their homelands and moved to government-owned areas called reservations.

By the late 1800s, the United States would cover the area south of Canada and north of Mexico, from the Atlantic Ocean to the Pacific Ocean.

After the gold rush of 1849, the population and landscape of the West was changed forever.

TRAVELED WEST ON THE OREGON TRAIL.

William Clark

**Thomas Jefferson** (1743–1826) was the third president of the United States. He hired Meriwether Lewis to lead an exploration of the land west of the Mississippi River. He was also the main author of the Declaration of Independence and served many roles in early American government.

**Toussaint Charbonneau** (ca. 1759–1843?) was a French Canadian fur trapper who lived among the Mandan and Hidatsa Indians. He was married to Sacagawea and served as an interpreter for the Corps of Discovery.

**William Clark** (1770–1838) led the Corps of Discovery along with Meriwether Lewis. He later served as governor of the Missouri Territory and as superintendent of Indian affairs.

**Patrick Gass** (1771–1870) was a member of the Corps of Discovery. He was promoted to sergeant on the expedition when Charles Floyd died. Gass was the first expedition member to publish his journals.

**Meriwether Lewis** (1774–1809) led the Corps of Discovery along with William Clark. He was a former army officer and served as President Thomas Jefferson's personal secretary.

Meriwether Lewis

**Sacagawea** (ca. 1786–1812) was the Shoshone wife of Toussaint Charbonneau. She was hired by Lewis and Clark to serve as an interpreter for the Corps of Discovery.

**Cameahwait** (? – ?) was the leader of the Lemhi Shoshone Indians and brother of Sacagawea.

Sacagawea

# TIMELINE

## 1803

**May 2**
The Louisiana Purchase is signed.

## 1804

**May 14**
The Corps of Discovery leaves St. Louis to begin the expedition.

**August 20**
Corps member Sergeant Charles Floyd dies from illness.

**September 25**
The corps meets the Teton Sioux Indians near what is now Pierre, South Dakota.

**October**
The corps arrives at the villages of the Mandan and Hidatsa Indians in what is now Bismarck, North Dakota.

## 1805

**April 25**
The corps arrives at the mouth of the Yellowstone River.

**Mid-June**
The corps is forced to portage around the Great Falls of the Missouri River.

**July 27**
The corps arrives at the Three Forks of the Missouri River, just south of what is now Helena, Montana.

**August 12**
Lewis finds the source of the Missouri River and crosses the Continental Divide. He realizes that a Northwest Passage does not exist.

**August 17**
The party arrives at the Shoshone camp; their leader, Cameahwait, is Sacagawea's brother.

**August 31**
The corps departs to cross the Bitterroot Mountains.

## 1804

**November**
Lewis and Clark hire French Canadian fur trapper Toussaint Charbonneau and his Shoshone wife, Sacagawea, as an interpreting team for the corps.

## 1804–1805

The corps camps with the Mandan and Hidatsa people for the winter.

## 1805

**February**
Sacagawea gives birth to Jean Baptiste Charbonneau.

**April 7**
Most of the corps continues to head west; a small number of corps members return east with specimens and messages from Lewis and Clark.

## 1805

**October 16**
The corps reaches the Columbia River.

**Mid-November**
The corps reaches the Pacific Ocean.

## 1805–1806

**Winter**
The corps camps at Fort Clatsop for the winter.

## 1806

**March 23**
The corps departs Fort Clatsop and heads for home.

**September 23**
The Corps of Discovery arrives back at St. Louis.

# LIVING HISTORY

Primary sources provide firsthand evidence about a topic. Witnesses to a historical event create primary sources. They include autobiographies, newspaper reports of the time, oral histories, photographs, and memoirs. A secondary source analyzes primary sources, and is one step or more removed from the event. Secondary sources include textbooks, encyclopedias, and commentaries. To view the following primary and secondary sources, go to www.factsfornow.scholastic.com. Enter the keywords **Lewis & Clark** and look for the Living History logo Σ¦.

Σ¦ **The Journals of the Corps of Discovery** Most of what we know about the Corps of Discovery's expedition comes from its members' journals.

Σ¦ **Meriwether Lewis's Letter to Thomas Jefferson**
Meriwether Lewis wrote a letter to President Thomas Jefferson on September 23, 1806, to inform him that the expedition had been a success.

Σ¦ **Thomas Jefferson's Letter to Congress** Westward exploration was one of Thomas Jefferson's major goals when he became president. He wrote a letter to Congress asking for funding for such an exploration.

Σ¦ **William Clark's Maps** William Clark's detailed maps of the Louisiana Purchase were a great help to the people who settled the new western lands.

# RESOURCES

## Books

Domnauer, Teresa. *Westward Expansion*. New York: Children's Press, 2010.

Ganeri, Anita. *On Expedition with Lewis and Clark*. New York: Crabtree Publishing, 2011.

Perritano, John. *The Lewis and Clark Expedition*. New York: Children's Press, 2010.

Pringle, Laurence P. *American Slave, American Hero: York of the Lewis and Clark Expedition*. Honesdale, PA: Calkins Creek Books, 2006.

**Visit this Scholastic Web site for more information on the Lewis and Clark Expedition: www.factsfornow.scholastic.com Enter the keywords Lewis & Clark**

# GLOSSARY

**Continental Divide** (kahn-tuh-NEN-tuhl di-VIDE) a line of high points of land in North America, which divides water that flows to the east from water that flows to the west

**estuary** (ES-chuh-wer-ee) the wide part of a river where it joins the ocean

**expedition** (ek-spuh-DISH-uhn) a long trip made for a specific purpose, such as for exploration

**frontiersman** (fruhn-TEERZ-muhn) a person who lives or works on land that has not been settled

**game** (GAME) wild animals hunted for sport or food

**gorge** (GORJ) a deep valley or ravine

**headwaters** (HED-wah-turz) the source of a stream or river

**interpreters** (in-TUR-prut-urz) people who translate a conversation between people who speak different languages

**keelboat** (KEEL-boht) a shallow covered riverboat that is usually rowed or poled

**moccasins** (MAH-kuh-sinz) soft, flat leather shoes

**pirogues** (PEE-rohgs) long boats that are similar to canoes

**portage** (PORT-ihj) to carry boats or goods overland around an obstacle

**sextant** (SEK-stuhnt) an instrument for measuring angular distances used in navigation

**species** (SPEE-sheez) a group of living things that have similar characteristics and can interbreed

**specimens** (SPES-uh-munz) samples or examples used to stand for a whole group

# INDEX

Page numbers in *italics* indicate illustrations.

# ABOUT THE AUTHOR

**Teresa Domnauer** is the author of many nonfiction books for children, including *Westward Expansion* and *Life in the West*, titles in Scholastic's True Books series. She has a bachelor of fine arts degree in creative writing from Emerson College and teaching certification from Ohio Dominican University. Domnauer lives in Fairfield, Connecticut, with her husband, Brendon, and their daughters, Ellie and Robin.